Occasional Hymns

Occasional Hymns

Poems

Paul Bowers

Turning Plow Press

Ringwood : Oklahoma

Acknowledgements

Some of the poems in this collection originally appeared in the following publications:

The Window Break, Boiled Eggs, An Oklahoma Weather Poem that Makes No Mention of Tornadoes, The Find, and Assurances appeared in *All Roads Will Lead You Home*; The Garden appeared in *Poetry Quarterly*; In Loving Memory appeared in *Concho River Review*; Apples of Gold appeared in *Red River Review*; Fleeing the Oklahoma Panhandle in Summer appeared in *San Pedro River Review*.

Copyright © 2018 Paul Bowers
All Rights Reserved.

Cover Design: Tim Kehn

ISBN: 978-0-692-15133-4

For Denise and Sydney

For Claudette Bowers (1931-2012)
'to make her smile'

and

E.C. Bowers
the song leader

Contents

I. *By-and-by*

By-and-By . . . 3
Fleeing the Oklahoma Panhandle in Summer . . . 4
I Shalopy Moo . . . 5
In Loving Memory . . . 7
The Old Chef's Home Helper . . . 8
Hymn for a Dead Battery . . . 9
A Prayer of Thanks Offered by Danny Gladwell
 at the Turpentine Bar, Lahoma, Oklahoma . . . 10
Feeding Agni . . . 11
The Find . . . 12
Predictions . . . 13
Aunt Billie, in Second Place . . . 14
The Keep . . . 15
The Sick Coyote and the County Deputy . . . 16
Assurances . . . 17

II. *Acre upon acre*

Witness . . . 21
An Oklahoma Weather Poem that Makes No Mention of
Tornadoes . . . 22
Calling Out . . . 23
A Portrait . . . 24
The Memory Stone . . . 25
Pilgrimage of the Cephalopods . . . 26
The Window Break . . . 27
Boiled Eggs . . . 28

Ideology . . . 29
The Garden . . . 30
A Definition of Wind . . . 31
A Dog's Life . . . 32
Old White Show Horse . . . 33
Coordinates . . . 34
Blueberry Skis the Kitchen Floor . . . 35
Two Lines in Snow . . . 36
Recall . . . 37

III. *The slow way we spell out answers*

Letter Blocks . . . 41
Apples of Gold . . . 42
Ouija . . . 43
Living Near the Tulsa International Airport . . . 44
The Last Lines . . . 45
Summer Vacation . . . 46
Pragmatism . . . 48
School Supply List . . . 49
The Kiln . . . 51
Reading the War Poets . . . 52
Headline: "Witness to Crime Devoured by Pigs" . . . 53
State Flu Deaths Double in a Week . . . 54
Retirement Speech . . . 56

I.

By-and-by

By-and-By

for Sanford Fillmore Bennett and Joseph P. Webster

When I was a child, how I loved the hymn
"The Sweet By-and-By," although I had
No idea what it meant, exactly, only
That we sang those sweet words on Sunday mornings
And sang about that beautiful shore where all hoped
To meet again someday. Later, when my father
Was very old, he told me of a fine saddle horse
He was forced to sell to the lumber company
Because he was a young man too poor to keep up the pretense
Of horse ownership, and then he told me
A horse that goes deep into the pines to pull logs
Never comes out again. It was the closest
He ever came to weeping over an animal, he said,
And in the round darkness of his eyes, in the tragic
Mask of his long expression, the by-and-by
Rose up and I saw that horse straining
Against the leather harness, and heard those singing chains.

Fleeing the Oklahoma Panhandle in Summer

after Steven Schroeder's painting Lot's Wife

Just to get her bearings in retreat
she throws a quick look back at the grain silos
pillared on the yellow flatscape of Guymon, Oklahoma

then she starts the toddlers
twin girls in mirrored car seats
on their boxed juices and saltines.

Her husband's spine stiffens
distracted hands resolve on the steering wheel
while the girls coo, soggy brine

and sweet grape on their tongues
ministered to by their mother
from the passenger seat.

She is almost alone with them
suddenly stilled by crossing those eternal distances
in the terror of July, in the time of falling fire.

I Shalopy Moo

> *They are like trees, planted by streams of water.*
> Psalm 1:3

Marched to in Selma, Alabama,
a sing-along with M.L. King, Jr.
crossing the Edmund Pettus Bridge,

then Pete Seeger's and Joe Glazer's version
singing for the Union—

We shall not be moved.

Played as a team chant
for the Leicester City Football Club
when it takes the field at King Power Stadium

and the walk-on song
for Shirley Crabtree
aka Big Daddy, the British grappler,
before a heavyweight wrestling match
against Giant Haystacks—

We shall not be,
we shall not be moved.

Closer to the heart
is Mississippi John Hurt
with his Delta blues guitar—

I shall not be moved

and Johnny and June
with a lively beat and tambourine—

Just like a tree planted by the waters

and my six-year-old sister
in Sapulpa, Oklahoma,
Emmanuel Missionary Baptist Church,
sometime in the mid-70s
testifying with odd
fruits of the spirit—

I shalopy, I shalopy moo.
I shalopy, I shalopy moo.

We confessed to one another at late Sunday supper
how such childish errors surely forced a smile
on the suffering criminal grimace of Jesus,
saved him from that silly burden of perfection,
his thirst quenched by a hymn of made-up words.

In Loving Memory

When you die
I will plant bloomed pink roses
On my hands and knees
Thorny stems clenched in my teeth.

When I die
Please feel free to drive my car.

When you die
I will mix aggregate and pozzolana
In the old Roman manner
And build a concrete bridge from this world
To the other with nothing but my bare hands
And river water fetched in my palms.

When I die
Don't forget to feed the dog, mow the lawn
And trim my lifeless hair.

When you die
I will fashion a roadside memorial
A circus of grief with trunkless elephants,
Humpless camels, and a carnival of crucifixes.

When I die
Make the memory of my body your pillow
Make my silence your cotton sheet
And get some sleep.

The Old Chef's Home Helper

It is of no use to paint your dining chairs
Spring green; they are, like you,
a splay of brittle spindles, crooked backs.

The round table in the kitchen alcove
is full of old vegetables in woven baskets
roasting naturally in the slower sunlight

and you without your favorite chopping knife,
your mind too dull to make them obedient for the skillet.
Yes, lunch will be no earlier or later than usual this winter

but the colder solstice is already upon you.
The morning light leaves the windowsill
to squat upon the baker's rack—

a golden cat, impatient to hold
back the day, descends to the floor
and seeks your aproned lap.

Hymn for a Dead Battery

My father's tongue was a slab of silent concrete
My mother's mind was a field of poppies
She pressed between her thoughts and kept
The cover closed. My sister's hands prayed
To emptiness and my brother's hands cracked
The necks of cats. Our car drizzled motor oil
Like black tree sap and ran flat-footed on old tires.
Somehow though we dodged the bullets of remorse
Kept most of our senses, learned to lean into
Our skin and last awhile. Then those translucent petals
Fluttered into my mother's lap one morning leaving us
To sweep up after her for a change. My father's
Aggregate tongue cracked in the cold of loneliness
And he said, though late, all the things he never said before
And then my sister said her faith was loose as her knee joints
And my brother crushed his grief in vices.
The leaking car, parked where the tree shed litter
On the day of my mother's funeral, lost its own will
In the night, and stubbornly refused to start.

A Prayer of Thanks Offered by Danny Gladwell at the Turpentine Bar, Lahoma, Oklahoma

Barrels shaped by long-
apprenticed coopers couldn't
hold liquor better than
my own rib cage.

As if I were made to drink, Lord,

as if I were *made for it.*

Dear God, you have blessed me.
You, the master cooper of my hoops
and staves. You, the hollower
of my gut so that I may be filled
as I see fit, and with what spirit fires
I choose, on any Friday. Hell,
on any Sunday.

Though not on Easter Sundays.
Not for me.

Not the next Easter, at least--
the one after this one.

Feeding Agni

In late March the news
is all about brushfires
and the occasional still-born calf—

the fire that was a controlled burn
turned loose, like the sin of Dante's seventh circle
carried up in a cinder. Fire that burns
in the hearts of those without prospects

and the slow digesting fire of Agni
to which the dead calf is offered
by a disappointed farm family

who with shovels gouge the red earth
open the wide dry mouth of sacrifice
stand back, and wait centuries
for the young bones to ignite.

The Find

The dog pinched a flattened rat carcass
from the sandy road
and held it hopefully until told
to leave it. He dropped the wallet of hair
then burst into a frantic run up the swell,
stopped to spin, chased his tail,
then off again
as if to say his offering,
though met with graceless disregard,
was not entirely lost on him.

Predictions

Too late to tell JFK
To shrug his shoulders
And sink into the seat.
Too late to tell MLK
To stay off the balcony
And ease his head cold in bed.
Too late to teach the Syrian boy
Who washed ashore
In Bodrum how to swim.

I have a country view
Windows that open to pastures
Time and distance as an excuse.
What floatation device
Can I toss into the past
That will not swell
Bob below the waves
And sink like guilt?

Aunt Billie, in Second Place

I don't remember you, Aunt Billie,
Beyond your bobbed hair
And the odd detail that came
From my mother that your neckbone
Once broke in your sleep,
Then you had chemotherapy
And your hair grew back curly.

But the notice from my eldest sister
That you had passed
Set me to counting aunts and uncles
On my fingers until I calculated
That you were the next to last,

That you were the penultimate—
The runner-up
Who barely misses out
On the blue ribbon
And the taller trophy.

One remains, whoever he or she is,
To take that prize
and end my reckonings.

The Keep

The white cathedral of the granary
absorbs the morning light and purifies it.

Belly full of breadstuff and given to long lulls
of concrete silences, it sleeps with the seasons,
stirred in June by late-Spring wheat
poured from an auger's iron gullet.

This is unleavened wealth,
riches cellared in fervent darkness
absent a requisite guardian dragon—

just Roy Berkshire, part-time night watchman,
with long-handled flashlight, a steady mug of instant coffee,

and the dutiful unnamed tabby cat,
tasked to frighten the smallest of night worshippers
that move from portal to hidden portal,
noses twitching with wild faith,
seeking slender entrance to the keep.

The Sick Coyote and the County Deputy

I watched the county deputy
walk around his flashing lights, gun drawn,
settling his cap then adjusting his pants
with his free hand, as if tightening his resolve
from the head down and pulling up his courage
with the weight of his ponderous belt.

The coyote, lean as a willow branch,
colorless as fog, lay curled against the bar ditch bank.
She didn't bother to lift her head out of respect
for the law, or raise her paws in surrender
or stuff a bit of out-of-season rabbit behind her back
or swallow the remnants of a farmyard hen.
She didn't even try to talk her way out of the jam
as coyotes sometimes do.
Instead, she bound herself into a ball
like a priceless stole.

The deputy waited until her eyes
were nearly closed then squinted
down the ice-gray barrel
of his service revolver. There he discovered
each strand of fur spun so thin and fine
that the bullet would barely stir a fiber
on its way to surprise her ailing heart.

Assurances

and one time he played
the banjo beneath an overpass
while we waited for a tow
into Alamogordo

and we, my brother and sister and I,
had the quilt palette
in the station wagon—
that aquarium of motion
and hot sleeps

and my mother fanning
herself with a Mesa Verde brochure
then digging saltines
from her mystical purse
to quiet her restless brood
who squawked over space
and music on the radio

and my father playing the banjo
on the shoulder of the interstate
beneath the overpass—
Old Joe Clark
and *Fisher's Hornpipe*
and *Cinch Mountain Backstep*—

and then when the tow truck arrived
to chain us to our rescue
to lift us out of our suffering
he picked *Blessed Assurance*
for his roadside finale.

I stopped chewing my crackers
and waited, instead, for the foretaste
of glory divine.

II.

Acre upon acre

Witness

When Rio Grande turkeys
Cross my vision
In a green pasture
Of winter wheat

You seem compelled to say
There is no such thing.
But it's true—
They parade in Spring, those

Balloons of feathers
Bowling balls in a strut
A rafter of passing shades.

Come look, if you don't believe.
Come to the window and look.

An Oklahoma Weather Poem that Makes No Mention of Tornadoes

In the rural wilds
the wind drives life away

by the fistful
by the dustful
by the leaful.

We are graveled
and wind groomed
cow blustered, horse gusted.

Know that our limbs bend
manes twist
dirt mangles;

know that the air
weaves and unravels
makes porch pots shatter.

The bob and wheel
of air moves us
lifts us, rhythms us

rhymes us. Who could live
in stillness, plainless
sweepless

without the bloom of a dirty sun
the angled stab in February
or the hot bent flame of June?

Calling Out

I could not help her
the woman who came to the door
late on a Saturday afternoon
with an iPhone photo of her missing dog.

"He's deaf," she said, "but answers to Stetson."

When the blind moonless night comes
she stands in the dark
along the shoulder of an empty highway
calling a name that cannot be heard
knowing how silly it is to shout for a dog
who will not come when called
who lives only through his eyes, nose,
and mute thrum of life in his paws.

Still she calls and calls
hands on her hips demanding obedience
until she no longer hears her own voice
raised by loneliness to such a pitch
only a dog can hear it.

A Portrait

The farmer's widow
slogs up the muddy path
to her faded farmhouse.
Rain has fallen lead-heavy for days
and blackened the roads and long blind curves.
She carries paper sacks full of two-week's groceries
totes the bags like justice weighed
along the walkway to her front door

while October leaves tremble on the boughs—
like waving, yellow-handed baboons
at a temple thousands of miles away.

The Memory Stone

The stone I found fits
perfectly in my hand
a red rock with a fluted waist
like an ancient mallet.
It is a bit of kitsch
on my desk, no flint
to chip, or bone
to break open
but long ago
I know I knew
how to lever it
with purpose, wedged in
a vee of wood
and dropped like a fist.
I keep it mostly within reach
a memory slightly beyond recovery
an inch beyond my fingertips.

Pilgrimage of the Cephalopods

Wearing bulbous heads
cat-eyed, shiny as apricot jelly
octopuses parade the evening beach
of New Quay, Ceredigion, Wales.

Shied by the prodding dry fingers
of half-frightened children
they wind and unwind their elastic arms
measuring distances like careful cartographers

over the sand
crawling inland

interested only in the coming nightfall
and the long-desired chance at a clearer view
of the always water-dimmed stars.

The Window Break

I see the break as a grown man
in the corner of his eye
suddenly recalls his fractured childhood;

as a surgeon examining a thin chest wound
finds the edges clean and sharp
but fears what might be accidently sewn inside
so near the victim's rose-colored heart.

The broken front window of my house
is an iceberg shard
set adrift above the box bushes outside.

From my desk chair
I look through the eyeglass skewed,
a permanent crack of enamel
on a bicuspid,
a dagger upright,
or a half-mountain of ice.

Sail-shaped and run aground,
a sloop in the cove of a sagging sea,
or a shark fin lifting from the sill
swimming slowly east.

I'll replace it some day
when I have nothing left to see,
like when the frozen river stops sliding
from the sharp leaning peak.

Boiled Eggs

A cracked egg boiled
pushes a mussel foot

from its oval
as if to get a grip on coral.

Clouds of white bloom
an elegant oleander in water.

I forgot the sequence:
eggs first in the pan, then water,

knowing full well eggs dropped
in anything fracture and ooze.

Still, to admire the ovum's blossom,
to love this hen's flower.

Ideology

The cardinals are back—
the red puddle of the male
and cloud-gray female
come to search
the dry yard of winter
to announce that green
is coming. But we don't believe
in the ambiguities of the halted
march of spring. Besides, winter
has become our habit
and to change our minds
too suddenly is to risk
the cramp of uncertainty.
Better to shoo the birds
by sending the dogs
running out the door
keep to our coats and gloves
and preserve those colder
comforts just a little while longer
than we know we should.

The Garden

There are always weeds,
those interlopers in my garden space
I think is a kind of Eden
and would contain only what
I have carefully poured from packets,
dropped into finger holes, covered
with a mist of dirt, then breathed
life into through the spout
of a neatly unwound garden hose.

When I leave for a few days,
on whatever dutiful journey
I have to take, I come back
to walk in the cool of the evening
to find those uninvited guests
again in rowdy trespass.

I feel no remorse at taking a hoe
and clearing them out, lopping off
their seedy heads or spading them up
until their feet are exposed.
Their bodies wither like
drying carcasses of headless snakes.

At times I dare to look beyond
the slatted garden wall,
up from my favored children
named Yellow Squash, Bush Beans,
Broccoli, and Rounding Melons,
toward the blue, uneven tree line to the east
where no ill-tempered demiurge
poisons and hacks to keep
heaven and hell apart,
but to witness, instead, the wild, errant acre
upon acre of untended paradise.

A Definition of Wind

e.g. the frantic branches of the elm
and the nervous sinew of powerlines
twitching between bone-stiff poles

also: a raucous head of long dark hair
or a sudden ballooning summer shirt

more at: the swaying bending shimmying
we sometimes see
the tossing buffeting pitching yaw
of daylight on water

more so: a transparent verb
a translucent name whispered

i.e. an invisible shouted complaint
of reluctant air called upon to reveal itself

cf. a conjured ghost
made to dance through smoke.

A Dog's Life

I ask the ancient dog
who stands at the window
what he is watching for

what has come into view;
"What sound draws you
so muzzle-close to the glass?" I ask.

I am right beside him
at my desk, in my chair
so he isn't waiting for me

but stares through the gnat-specked pane
as if what is on the way
is well worth yearning for.

Later I find him asleep on the floor
beneath the windowsill
the light gone blind outside

and having forgotten the entire episode.
Even if he could reply he would say
that he had no clear memory
of waiting for anything,

then refuses to acknowledge
that I ever questioned him
about such a silly thing.

Old White Show Horse

A white horse who lacks all nobility
propping herself on bad hips and weak hocks
was once the mount of a princess
before the princess grew and left home
and the horse was given to age.

Now a pasture mare
rarely saddled with a chore
useless in her late mode
yet full of slow breath, slow motion
and sacred in her own right.

Coordinates

I have measured the long
Dry branches of January.

I have accounted for
The shifting clouds of geese

That lift and roll above
The green whiskers of winter wheat.

I have acknowledged the cat
That warms like gravity in my lap.

I have figured out where winter is centered:
In the earth's lazy tilt

In the movement of razored air
In the southernmost sunlight

In the deep bone chill.
And it rides over the horizon,

Like a knight in mail—
Cold, stiff, but determined.

Blueberry Skis the Kitchen Floor

Imagine a skier running on slatted feet,
tree slabs buckled and stiff to boots, poles in hand to stab
and paddle the powder for balance.

Blueberry, the cat, partially paralyzed and ski-footed in the rear,
is a planker, carving edges on his flat metatarsals,
a ripper thumping around the kitchen in the morning
on the first run of the day, the "milk run" as the ski pros call it.
He slaloms chair legs and human legs, noodles to his food bowl
across the hardpack of cold linoleum,
this cat come to live at our snowless house,
who downhills his life away.

Two Lines in Snow

To disappear—
Without being dead, of course—

Is more like signing off
Or forging a fake name

Denuded
Like a jungle after napalm

Or to refuse to walk outside
During a snowstorm

Although what falls
Would quickly cover the typewriter hops of birds

Human tracks are too mortal
To die so quietly in the squall.

Recall

A shoe's soles are memories of walks and quiet closets
Seeds are silent hymns to leaf and root, flood and drought

Your hair curls without effort like a vine round a familiar trunk
I remember my grandfathers' thoughts when I am quiet and listen

I often dream the dreams of others
Like detached motion pictures

I watch from a chair in the kitchen.
The body recalls its long history

Before it was a body, before
Life found it and put it on

For safekeeping. Before that
It was lichen on a stone

A fish in the shallows waiting
For the tremble of a fallen insect

Before that, recall that bend
Of light curving round a planet.

III.

The slow way we spell out answers

Letter Blocks

My mother disturbs my sleep
with kindness
a comforting spirit
who would visit me—

that lovely Missionary
Baptist woman—

not to say anything
only to make herself
known in memory.

I never note
her voice, only witness
her shade in the shadows
of my childhood

where I am forever reaching out
to stack one letter block
upon another
to make her smile.

Apples of Gold

Mrs. Perryman, fifth-grade teacher,
chalked lines from *Apples of Gold*
on the board every morning.

We copied them with diligence
letter by letter
until we had a collection
of sayings to live by:

ancient and practical
jolts of kindness doled out to children
as a morning exercise in proper penmanship.

What beautiful sentiments
must have lined the insides
of the giant garbage bins
when school was let out at year's end
and all the desks were cleared,
those hollow mouths swept clean
of half pencils and paperless crayons
and abandoned spiral notebooks.
Imagine those words roiling—
entries in a lottery,
turned round and round—
and those few scraps that blew
into the world as fragments of wisdom
cribbed by long vanished schoolchildren.

Ouija

On an elementary playground
I was informed that 55 years
would mark my end, a fate
spelled out by ghostly hands
that moved mine around the board,
and those of my best friend, Johnny,
our fourth-grade fingers bunched lightly
on the planchette near its clear, glass eye.

Johnny was going to be the heroic Marine,
the spirits revealed over lunchtime recesses,
then a running back for the Rams,
then President of the United States.

I, on the other hand, would likely croak mid-life
holding down a meaningless job,
an aging bachelor, childless, bankrupt.

I suspect Johnny had learned to cheat at Ouija.

Yet I still check our hometown newspaper's obituary page
more than four decades on
to see if his name appears before mine
while I count the nervous hours to my 56th
shadowed by two boys hunched over a Hasbro game,

knowing nothing, then or now,
of the slow way we spell out answers
with an arc of letters, bold Noes and Yeses,
a series of numbers, one to zero,
and a final, bottom-of-the-board, *Good Bye.*

Living Near the Tulsa International Airport

Aircraft chalk-mark the
slate of sky.

I have waited too long to look up
to read what was written
there

and see only drifting smudges
smeared by wind.

But I'm sure it was about love
or birds or the dead—
those words that live on high
we sometimes squint
into the sunlight to witness.

Tomorrow I'll lug a chair
into the yard

put on my reading glasses, tilt back my head,
draw pen and pad from my coat pocket,

and ready myself for that first
strike of white, and the slight
delayed slash of sound that
speaks what is written.

The Last Lines

I can only see him as
a Holocaust survivor—
although he is not Jewish

he is from Brooklyn
and has that Jewish baker
about him.

My wife's father
in his bird-gray skin
is flying to

his conclusion
like a poem that begins
with crude comparison

then collapses into the flesh
of an old man
writing his last lines.

Summer Vacation

We dug potatoes instead of going to Disneyland.
We dug potatoes by hand, a full acre of sandy loam,
although a thousand hectares it seemed in the heat,
our feet blistering in high muck boots,
hands coated in grit, fingernails packed with soil,
backs prying up roots with potato spades,
dragging thick buckets from row to row to row
then dumping the hard russets
into the garden cart.

Instead of vacation at the beach
we picked our own peaches
at a Porter orchard because the store-bought
or the pre-picked tumbled into bushel baskets
and ready for sale under the big green awning
were just not sweet in my mother's mouth,
so my father, eternally in love with her,
drove us two hours to the U-Pick Grove,
aluminum ladder slung like a crucifix
on top of the van, pinioned with cotton ropes.

We spent the day in trees, like golden marmosets,
dropping peaches in pouches
made by ballooning our shirts.

Instead of a tour of Paris on motorbikes
we pulled corn, our hands sticky with starch, corn silk in our hair,
an errant earworm discovered glued to someone's neck
long after we left the field—
then hours of shucking into paper sacks.

Instead of walking the Great Wall
we rolled cantaloupes onto the garden path
for our sisters to lift, sniff for ripeness, then load.

Instead of the Riviera
we picked okra and itched for days.

Instead of the Royal Gorge,
we plumbed deep vines for sugar snap peas.

Instead of Christmas in Quebec City,
or Lapland, or even New York,
instead of ski trips to Santa Fe
my mother folded her arms and wistfully surveyed
the dwindling cache of canned peaches and corn.

Dad, knowing the signs, took down the seed catalogue,
spread it on the kitchen table like De Soto's map,
closed his eyes, and pointed at a page.

We gathered round to see into distant summer,
and where we weren't going next.

Pragmatism

This poem boils potatoes
Fixes flat tires
Helps you find your car keys.

It relaxes tense bowels.

It will make things happen.

Like this: a tree maturing against
An old fencepost
In a farmyard
Until
The post and tree
Dance together, indistinguishable,
Which is this wood,
And which is that wood
And how we can't know
Which is
And which is not
But be satisfied
In our practical ignorance.

School Supply List

2 Pink Erasers (severed badger tongues)
1 Box Permanent Colored Markers (childhood scars that will never heal)
1 Bottle White Glue (the milk sap of youth)
1 3-ring Binder (rib bones in flayed skin)
1 Box of Tissues (white gulls that glide about the eyes)
6 Number 2 Pencils (yellow totems of the smallest tribe)
4 Quart-sized Freezer Bags (gall bladders for papier-mâché tears)
1 Spiral Notebook, Wide-Ruled (a barbwired room, with blue ceiling and blue floor)
1 Pair Safety Scissors (a mind blunted by anxiety)
1 Box Crayons (wax torpedoes in a launch tube)

Additional items might include:

>   a much-loved stuffed bear,
>   a photo of the ocean,
>   a snip of the family cat's fur,
>   a list of obscure allergies,
>   a short cautionary tale about boys,
>   seven methods of reaching at least one parent,
>   and a detailed map home in case of:
>>   a medical emergency,
>>   a general dissatisfaction with First Grade,
>>   a failed attempt at holding hands,
>>   a playground punch to the nose,
>>   a sudden breakthrough in math,
>>   the untimely death of Santa Claus
>>   or the murder of the Easter Bunny,
>>   both by that mean kid, Joseph Roy,
>>   who lives just down the road;
>>   a scuffed knee
>>   a slightly sprained ankle
>>   an embarrassing lack of athletic ability
>>   a shoe that won't stay tied

a word you don't understand
a problem you can't solve
or a disappointed heart that finds
it cannot beat so quietly as before
you ate your breakfast
of cereal and buttered toast,
gathered all your school supplies,
and fell into the world
just outside our front door.

The Kiln

The first thing I ever ordered
was a regular boy's haircut
from Bill the Barber,
in Prattville, Oklahoma,

and the second thing
I ever ordered was a rainbow sno-cone
from the shop next door.
I walked to the barber alone
with real money in my pocket.

Then, freshly trimmed, and still itching
under the ghost of the white paper collar,
I ordered that rainbow sweetness
in a conical cup, and walked Mohawk Avenue

toward home, past the ceramics shop
where my siblings and I collected discards,
like malformed bones born harmed
from the kiln and left for the taking:

a chalky elephant missing its trunk,
a one-winged angel,
a clown head absent a round nose—

Today, I saw that Syrian boy on TV,
sitting in an ambulance seat in Aleppo—

hair wild with rubble and rainbow blood,
forehead blooming a bomb burst clown nose:

a boy left too long in the kiln,
though with trunk and wings intact,
and waiting to be taken home.

Reading the War Poets

I will never lob concussive metaphors
shell-shocked nouns
trench-deep verbs
images thick as chlorine gas
nor unwind barbed analogies
in deadly curls across the barren page

the likes of which Sassoon, Brooke, and Owen
with their authentic bloodied vowels
cannoned exclamations
word grenades
released from their muddied hands
to burst in our ears, explode in our mouths.

Headline: "Witness to Crime Devoured by Pigs"

I've had rough days:
late for work and the gut hit
of a flat tire in the driveway,
or sudden vomit and fever,
or an angry note on a Walmart receipt
after a night of argument.

But to be eaten by hogs,
Duroc and Yorkshire;

to be roughly lifted over the thick wire panels
made to keep pigs at home, and apart;
to be enthusiastically dismantled,
fingers and toes, the crunchier bits first, I suppose;
the erasure of nipples, clipped bangs, earlobes,
then through the thick skin of the belly
for the delectable sweetbreads.

Connoisseurs of mud and moldy loaves
and leftovers scraped from farmhouse dinner plates.

The farm family just finished
a big meal, so the youngest boy
totes the offal at dusk
to the pen and drops
the slop into the trough, unawares,

which the hogs, by now too important
for their own good, ignore.

They'll be mentioned in *The Farm News,*
connected to suspicious criminal activity by morning,
though eventually found innocent of all charges.

State Flu Deaths Double in a Week

- Cough
- Sore throat
- Headaches
- Body aches
- Chills
- Fever
- Fatigue

Beware, those who are young
Those elderly or pregnant, those with
Compromised immune systems

Those driving older model sedans
Those who take more than their fair share
Those who sometimes fail to wash their hands
Those who skate on morally thin ice
Those with poorly parted hair

Who merge late into the single lane at road construction sites
With more credit debt than common courtesy
With more burger on their plates than broccoli
Who have more Schnauzer in their blood than Collie.

The best protection is to have the most up-to-date vaccination.
Barring that, may the CDC recommend certain pilgrimage destinations?

Lourdes for a quick bath and healing gulp
Or Medjugore for a virus-suppressing apparition of Mary

For those with heavy mucus
Try the Mother Ganges at Benares

Or Glastonbury to draw deep
From Arthur's Chalice Well

Or, if you can swing the fare
The Western Wall in Jerusalem
That ruined temple of hope and despair.

If, however, the symptoms occur
Within a few days of infection
Tamiflu and ibuprofen will often suffice
Just as well as miracles.

Retirement Speech

Let me just say:

I filched 243 ink pens over the years.
I stowed blended scotch in the file cabinet under N for "necessary."
I was the one who left the tuna sandwich in the lounge fridge for five weeks
and ate the fresh homemade pasta you bragged about in the red bento box
and drank half the Dr. Pepper on the top rack you said you *so* looked forward to,
then put the opened can back.

The fractured computer mouse in the workroom?
The waffled boot prints on the conference table?
The perpetually disappearing ream of paper from the supply closet?
The goldfish floating belly up in the office tank?
The rolling chair missing a wheel you were not warned about?
The tape dispenser you found in the women's toilet?
The desk phone you found on the roof?
The fourteen dollars missing from the employee sympathy flower fund jar?

All me.

The door dings on your new car
(which you noticed)
and the "Kick me" sticky note on your back
(which you didn't)?
The joke valentine that hurt your feelings,
the joke lottery ticket that got your hopes up?

Also me.

And the time I sneezed into my hand then turned around, smiled, and shook yours and cost you five sick days?

Sorry for that.

And it was me who left you a hundred dollar bill because you
needed to keep your apartment
and me who stuffed the comments box with notes of praise
and got you a raise,
and me who left the flowers on the grave
of your youngest daughter
then three weeks later
gave you a two out of ten rating
for poor work ethic and inattention to detail.

Friends, fellow employees, comrades, enemies, jerks, my worst
nightmares;
those I envy, adore, despise;
those I've talked about and ignored,
lied to, learned from, stolen from, damaged, and denied:

here are all my office keys
a spare box of paperclips
a never-used three-hole punch
an unopened stack of Dixie cups.

Here is my handshake
my hit-the-road thumb
my middle-finger adieu.

Here is my wink
my stuck-out tongue
my departing shot
my primal scream
my death rattle
my last smug look
my final knowing nod
my concluding ambiguous stare

that shows you all how little
and how much I truly care.

About the author

Paul Bowers lives and writes in the rural wilds of northwest Oklahoma. Other book-length works include a collection of short fiction, *Like Men, Made Various* (Lost Horse Press) and a poetry collection, *The Lone, Cautious, Animal Life* (purple flag press). Visit *paulbowers.org* for additional information about the author, ordering books, or to schedule a reading.

Turning Plow Press

Ringwood : Oklahoma

www.ingramcontent.com/pod-product-compliance
Lightning Source LLC
Chambersburg PA
CBHW032050290426
44110CB00012B/1030